Annie Herring

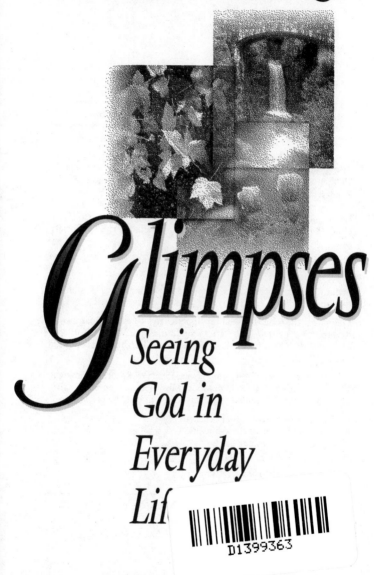

Glimpses

Seeing God in Everyday Life

BETHANY HOUSE PUBLISHERS
MINNEAPOLIS, MINNESOTA 55438

Glimpses
Copyright © 1996
Annie Herring

All scripture quotations, unless indicated, are taken from the HOLY BIBLE, NEW INTERNATIONAL VERSION®. Copyright © 1973, 1978, 1984 by International Bible Society. Used by permission of Zondervan Publishing House. All rights reserved. The "NIV" and "New International Version" trademarks are registered in the United States Patent and T ademark Office by International Bible Society. Use of either trademark requires the permission of International Bible Society.

Scripture quotations marked NASB are from the New American Standard Bible, © The Lockman Foundation 1960, 1962, 1963, 1968, 1971, 1972, 1973, 1975, 1977.

Scripture quotations marked KJV are from the King James Version of the Bible.

Lyrics from the song "Here on the Sphere," *Flying Lessons*, Sparrow Records. Copyright © 1989 Latter Rain Music/Midi Mouse Music (Admin. by EMI Christian Music Publishing). All rights reserved. Used by permission.

Lyrics from the song "Purify Me," *Hymns*, Sparrow Records. Copyright © 1989 Latter Rain Music/Midi Mouse Music (Admin. by EMI Christian Music Publishing). All rights reserved. Used by permission.

Published by Bethany House Publishers
A Ministry of Bethany Fellowship, Inc.
11300 Hampshire Avenue South
Minneapolis, Minnesota 55438

Printed in the United States of America.

Library of Congress Cataloging-in-Publication Data

Herring, Annie.
  Glimpses : seeing God in everyday life / Annie Herring.

ISBN 1–55661–745–3

Applied for

Contents

Foreword

I always associate the beginning of my acquaintance with Annie Herring with my old, blue, dilapidated Volkswagen. The car was a virtual shambles—only impressive in that it was unimpressive, and only remembered because it somehow marked a special time and place.

It was the era of the Jesus People. The place was southern California. It was a time when cars of every shape, make and model bore bumper stickers reading, "Honk If You Love Jesus." And the area echoed with horn blowing.

It was a time when God transformed the hearts of hippies, druggies and devotees of everything from LSD to heroin to acid rock music. The splendor of divine grace was everywhere, and people were getting saved! I mean, *really* transformed—flooded with tidal waves of divine love.

That was the climate, and I was a happy victim of this sunshine from heaven, as God beamed an incredible display of grace into a little chapel in Van Nuys, California, called The Church On The Way.

When Buck and Annie Herring walked in to church one Sunday morning, I didn't even notice Annie at first. When I saw Buck's towering physique and almost fearsome visage—with bearded face and long hair—I had to compose myself before I could greet him properly. Meanwhile, slight, sweet Annie disappeared in his shadow.

But it wasn't long before both Buck and Annie (as well as Matthew and Nellie, Annie's brother and sister) became the dearest of friends. I experienced what I believe is the dearest relationship a person can know outside of marriage—to be called "pastor" by people who truly love you as their God-given shepherd in Christ.

I made regular pastoral calls on the Herrings. The fact is, I called as much for my sake as theirs, because no matter how brief the visit, I never left without being refreshed by something Annie shared.

The scenario was almost always the same. I'd arrive in the old blue VW, we'd all have a round of hugs, and a snack would be prepared. Soon, without pretentiousness, or self-promotion, Buck would say, "Hey, let me share something we found in the Word this morning, and the Lord gave Annie a song to go with it!"

Within a few years, many of those "words from His Word" became songs that were sung around the world, by "2nd Chapter of Acts."

Annie's joy and release in knowing the living Jesus tenderly and poignantly overflowed in song after song. The hallmark of her music was its holy candor and gentle openness to God's presence and love. Her spirit saw the heart of God, then transmitted that vision through her fingers as she played, and her voice as she sang. Jesus always seemed nearer and dearer to me whenever Annie sang.

When I was asked to write a few words introducing *Glimpses*, all of this came to mind. But my purpose here isn't simply to wax nostalgic, but to introduce a *person*.

The lady who writes on these pages is what I call an "unmystical mystic." By that I mean that she doesn't conduct herself in a mysterious way or act as though she just arrived from another planet. But she does see the invisible as few do. She gains glimpses—then relates what she sees in a way that helps others see God's heart as never before.

Annie Herring conveys the sincerity of unspoiled simplicity, born out of a depth of love. As Jesus said, "Those who have been forgiven much, love much." The fragments of her past have caught the glory-light of heaven, providing us all with fresh views of "the manifold wisdom of God" (Eph. 3:10).

One of my all-time favorite "Buck and Annie memories" took place in the springtime, over two decades ago. My old blue car bounced to a stop, I was through the front door of the Herring home and a snack was on the coffee table. For the umpteenth time Buck said, "Ya gotta hear what the Lord gave Annie yesterday." She started to play and sing, "Hear the bells ringing, they're singing that you can be born again!" The old upright rocked as she swayed back and forth, with eyes closed and head lifted heavenward. "Easter Song" had been born!

I get teary every time I hear it, not only because the song's dynamic statement of everlasting joy moves me, but because I am drawn back to those days of revival, that time when the "new wine" of the Holy Spirit flowed so freely.

But I assure you, the Winemaker still lives. And when hearts keep open to Him, He shows up today to serve the newest wine. And as He did so long ago, He often saves the best for last.

In Annie Herring, you will find a heart that is truly genuine, childlike and simple, receiving the "new wine" that is still being served to her daily.

So it is in *Glimpses*. You are about to catch a new vision. The Holy Spirit is still doing that, you know. He's still causing people who drink deeply to catch a glimpse of his grace.

Come taste the wine. And be uplifted by what its newness will help you see.

Pastor Jack Hayford
The Church On The Way
Van Nuys, California

About Annie

Annie Herring is one of those rare devotional writers whose creativity is charged by her touching, honest, electrifying, sweet and solid intimacy with the Creator. The force within her words is the force of a soul abandoned in the worship of One she loves. But you will know this already if you have heard 2nd Chapter of Acts, the musical trio whose name was synonymous with the passionate devotion of Christian music lovers.

Though Acts remains a legend in contemporary Christian music, many do not know how this group—comprised of Annie and her two gifted siblings, Matthew and Nellie—came together out of tragedy.

Annie, Matthew, and Nellie were three of nine children born to the Wards, itinerant farmers in rural North Dakota. Though the Wards couldn't afford luxuries like indoor plumbing, a bright spirit of love, fun, and devotion to God buoyed them through many hard times. Music, which included family singing, was a big part of their lives. At five, Annie began singing at farm co-op meetings and country church picnics with two older sisters, their mother accompanying them on the piano.

During these early years, Annie experienced an overwhelming sense of the transcendent beauty, power, and glory of God in the quiet worship of the country church where her family attended.

Annie left North Dakota to pursue a career in music in Los Angeles in the 1960's. The rock music scene had taken the world by storm, and with it the culture of drugs and "free love." In short order, Annie had fallen in with top songwriters and pop music stars. While her amazing voice carried her to the brink of stardom, her lifestyle carried her toward inner despair.

Annie felt a major blow when her mother died of a brain tumor in 1968. Reeling inside, she began to explore Eastern mysticism and New Age religion, searching for relief from her pain. About this time, her boyfriend, Buck—an L.A. deejay—surrendered his life to Christ through the invitation of a former drug dealer. After this experience, Buck began to see the huge gap between his new beliefs and the music he played on the air. He couldn't help but be troubled at the influence the lyrics and spirit of rock music was having on the young people who heard it.

Buck began praying for Annie and introduced her to the Bible. At first she resisted, but one day, while at the piano, words and music came to her out of the blue. Where had it come from? she thought. Suddenly, in her mind's eye, it was as if Jesus were walking toward her, and the conviction came that the music was a gift from Him. He seemed to say, *The only thing I ask is that you give your life to Me and let Me live through you.*

Then came a terrible struggle in Annie's spirit. Her lifestyle had led her into spiritual darkness and caused her to do things for which she felt deeply ashamed. One day, as a group of Christians placed their hands on her to pray, the anguish became so great she bolted from the room. That night, she sobbed into her pillow, feeling that she had placed herself beyond the reach of God's forgiveness. She fell asleep asking, "How could You love me. . . ?"

But as the light of a new morning shone through her bedroom window, Annie woke with new words on her lips—a prayer filled with amazement and hope: *How could You love me so much?* In that moment of surrender, she experienced the presence of the risen Christ for the first time . . . and her life would not be the same.

Not long afterward,˙ Annie's father died, leaving Annie's youngest brothers and sister orphaned. Matthew was twelve, and Nellie fourteen, when they came to California to live with Annie and her new husband, Buck Herring. It wasn't long before Matthew and Nellie surrendered their lives to Christ, too.

About this time, Buck met Barry McGuire, a rock star

whose song, "Eve of Destruction," had been a major hit. McGuire had also become a Christian and was singing and sharing his faith with young people. One night Buck asked Annie, Matthew, and Nellie to gather around the old upright and treat McGuire to an impromptu concert.

Annie had sensed that God was saying: *You, Nellie, and Matthew will sing as one voice.* When Barry McGuire heard them sing that evening, he thought they sounded like angels.

It wasn't long before 2nd Chapter of Acts was born. For two decades, the group was a musical phenomenon, performing and recording with such Christian music greats as Phil Keaggy and Michael O'Martian. Annie's simple tune "Easter Song" became an instant contemporary classic. The call to ministry was always the same: "To see the body of Christ healed, and to see people's needs met. There is hope in Jesus. There is no situation too great for Him to resolve."

"All we ever wanted," the Herrings say today, "was for people to see Jesus. We only wanted to hear Him say, 'Well done, good and faithful servants.' " And so, at the height of success, when they believed God was leading them to stop recording, the only faithful response was to obey.

Annie has continued to minister as a well-loved solo artist, and several years ago at a Christian Booksellers Convention, 2nd Chapter of Acts regrouped briefly to sing three worship songs, bringing the thousands who were in attendance into a sense of the holiness of God. Afterward, a well-known man of God approached them—not to praise their musical greatness but to say, "The *frame* never outdid the *picture*."

"That was our earnest desire in all we did," Annie and Buck conclude, "that the frame would *never* outdo the picture. And the picture had to be *Jesus*."

1
Glimpses

*Now we see but a poor reflection as in
a mirror; then we shall see face to face.
Now I know in part; then I shall know
fully, even as I am fully known.*

1 CORINTHIANS 13:12

I have a glimpse now—where a couple of months
ago I had none. What happened? Did time make my
heart grow stronger? Was it commitment? Do vows
we make in life really work?

Before God they do! For He is a partner in our
vows—invisible, sometimes unfelt, but always
there. And He is always faithful! So because of this
promise from Him, I know He has brought me
through and held my hope when it blew out of my
sails. And He has been blowing back that hope so
gently. At first I couldn't even feel it, but now I
have a glimpse.

And oh what you can do with just a glimpse!

The sliver of a moon sometimes does more for
me than a full one. It must be that it reminds me of
my life here on earth ... just a sliver of time, just a

glimpse of light. But soon all time will stand still and be in full light. Oh, how I long for that full light! For the completion of my race, for my spirit to be finally dislodged from this body—even though through it I have enjoyed God's creation and seen the beauty He has made on the earth and the expanse in the heavens.

How much more awaits me? What more will I see?

Every time I think I've seen it all, I turn a corner and another chapter of the story unfolds. I never get tired of this life; I still enjoy things as if seeing them for the first time. And maybe that's why I need to see the sliver of the moon—to remind me of all that is to come, all that is so much greater than this life on this beautiful earthly sphere.

But it is easy for us to get hung up on the immediate, or get caught up with our own needs. So we end up with major problems, in society and in our lives, that reflect our selfishness. And the attitude of "I deserve better" or "I deserve to be happy" prevails over our vows of commitment.

People didn't always think they deserved so much; they were more likely to work things out. They were stronger in their commitments when they found someone to love who loved them in return. You can get a lot of mileage in a relationship based on a disciplined commitment that nurtures hope.

Now we feel more, sin more, expect more, need more, want more . . . more . . . more. We walk in a world of pretend and lies cultivated by advertising, television and movies. And because of our lack of commitment, we end up honoring people whose deeds are dishonorable, exposing things that shouldn't be exposed, and laughing with sarcastic humor that devalues other humans.

God forgives a lot each day: wrong deeds, sins done in darkness, attitudes that violate the principles of righteousness, abusive words and violent acts. This wrong and all wrong-doing He took on Himself in one day. No wonder the heart of God—that very powerful heart of love—broke.

Forgive me, Father, for wrong actions and attitudes. Help me see the light shining through your broken heart that gives me a glimpse of hope and love and grace. May that glimpse empower me to do your will. Amen.

My personal reflections

_____

_____

_____

_____

_____

_____

_____

_____

2
"You, You, You"

Unless you change and become like little children, you will never enter the kingdom of heaven.

MATTHEW 18:3

Recently, as I listened to my car radio, an old song came on that I hadn't heard for years. It stayed with me because I used to sing that song to my nephews when they were little:

You, you, you. I'm in love with you, you, you.

Since those were the only words I ever remembered, I made up more words that fit the moment, and it became "our song."

Hearing that song after all these years took me back to my childhood and the childhood of my nephews. And I cried, because I missed my "little" nephews who are now all grown up. I thought about how time passes, how quickly things change.

Then I thought, God isn't ruled by time as we know it. He still values my childhood—a part of my life that continues to shape who I am today. He sees the whole picture.

When past sin pops into my head I usually say, Hey, wait a minute . . . you're redeemed—let it go. But if the nagging persists, sometimes it is my loving Father bringing those things to mind to help me understand the root of sin, so that the child within me will be set free from guilt and fear through confession and absolution. He does this to enable me to be all I am to be.

No doubt you've seen the bumper sticker that asks, "Have you hugged your kid today?" Do you dare to look at that little person within you that still may be bruised and say, "I love you, I understand," and let the comfort of Christ hold the child within?

To be childlike is not for a chosen few, but for each one of us. The beginning of freedom is sitting in the lap of our Heavenly Father, and allowing ourselves to be held by Him. Have you had your hug today?

Thank you, Father, for your tenderness towards me. I'll sit in your lap, rest in your arms, until I fully recognize how much you love me. Amen.

My personal reflections

_____

_____

_____

_____

_____

_____

_____

_____

_____

_____

_____

_____

_____

_____

_____

_____

_____

_____

_____

_____

3
Silent Keepers

Lift up your eyes on high and see who has created these stars! The one who leads forth their host by number, He calls them all by name. Because of the greatness of His might and the strength of His power, not one of them is missing.

ISAIAH 40:26 (NASB)

When you feel lost or discouraged, look up—you'll see stars, the silent keepers of God's Word. And oh how magnificently they display His glory! It is not by chance that they are lights burning brightly, held in a dark expanse—for they are an example of how we are to shine. We are all God's creation, intended to reflect His eternal light. But the silent keepers are numbered by the Mighty One and called by name. How I love their panorama. At times I feel I can hear them ringing the symphony of God's light, breaking the night silence with the song of the Bright and Morning Star!

Here on this beautiful sphere,
Looking upward we gaze

As the beauty amazes
the mind—

There's not one of a kind;
Not a one is the same,

And they each have a name;
Giving light all through
the night,

Giving sight a constant flight.

Here in the dance of the skies
Twinkling planets arise,
Making music that flies
without sound—
Barely touching the ground;
Living silence resounds,
Bringing to the earthbound
Living light all through
the night,
Giving sight a constant light.

May my life be like the stars to bring hope to those
who live in darkness and light to their pathway. May I
reflect your glory, my Creator, and share the song you
have placed within my heart. Amen.

My personal reflections

_____

_____

_____

_____

_____

_____

_____

_____

_____

_____

_____

_____

_____

_____

_____

_____

_____

_____

_____

_____

_____

4
My Tree

Blessed is the man [who] delights in the Law of the Lord . . . He is like a tree planted by streams of water, which yields its fruit in season and whose leaf does not wither. Whatever he does prospers.

PSALM 1:1–3

I enjoy watching the grand old oak tree outside my bedroom window. It clothes itself in green each spring and then discards its worn-out clothes in the fall.

The oak depends on the wind to come and blow away the old leaves. I, too, depend on the wind of God's Spirit to blow through me, to get rid of the old so I will be ready for the spring in my soul.

My tree always has company; no matter how it looks, it's never lonely. The birds depend on my tree. Some just for a moment as they migrate in the fall and return to the north in the spring. But others have made it their permanent home.

And the squirrels love my oak tree all year long. They wait for the acorns to grow so they can store them for the winter. In the spring they spread themselves out on a limb, warming themselves in the sun. Woodpeckers beat on the trunk to get the bugs out, and although the tree must not appreciate it at the time, it grows stronger by being rid of the pests.

I want to be more like my tree—to offer a safe place for others to find rest and bask in the sun, to gather fruit and grow in strength. To be as gracious as my tree when others come to get the "bugs" out.

And during those times when I am weary in well-doing, I gently am reminded that Jesus stretched out His arms on a tree.

I've watched that oak tree that stands outside my bedroom window for only a year and a half. Yet that tree grew for many years without anyone admiring it or noticing its beauty.

If only I could do the same.

By observing your creation, Lord, we get a glimpse of you. May I be a nurturing oak today to those you have placed in my life. Amen.

My personal reflections

_____

_____

_____

_____

_____

_____

_____

_____

_____

_____

_____

_____

_____

_____

_____

_____

_____

_____

_____

5
Time Off

*Find rest, O my soul, in God alone; my
hope comes from him.*

PSALM 62:5

One of the hardest times in my life was when
2nd Chapter of Acts stopped touring. Throughout
the twenty years of singing with my brother and
sister, Matthew and Nelly, I had the joy of knowing
God's faithfulness.

But then God said something new to each one
of us. And because of His faithfulness through the
years, I knew I could trust Him completely with
their future and mine. Although I wasn't clear on
everything, I knew I was to take time off. And deep
inside I thought, *Aha! Now I finally get to do those
things I never could do while I was on the road.*
Things like baking, visiting my neighbors, having
days without interruption to study God's Word,
being a homemaker, and fulfilling those dreams
I had put on the shelves of tomorrow so I could
minister today.

Here I was, finally free from the obligations of travel, concerts and recordings. Yet, even though I had the time I didn't do any of the things I had planned. And I began to feel guilty, asking myself: *What's wrong with me? Why can't I take advantage of this wonderful opportunity and fill up my time with the things of the Lord?*

As I chastised myself for my lack of discipline, I felt the Lord speak to me again. He showed me that I had misunderstood His direction to take "time off." Instead, He wanted me to take the framework of "time" off of our relationship and simply love Him!

How freeing for me to realize that the Lover of my soul does not require me to punch a time clock in my quest of spirituality. Instead, I accomplish His will for my life by loving Him and making Him my heart's focus.

Infinite God beyond time, help me slow down and savor the moments of life we share together, to exult in the unspeakable gift of loving you. Amen.

My personal reflections

_____

_____

_____

_____

_____

_____

_____

_____

_____

_____

_____

_____

_____

_____

_____

_____

_____

_____

_____

6
Raindrops

Blessed are those who hunger and thirst for righteousness, for they will be filled.

*Raindrops falling, landing,
being absorbed by the thirsty ground.
The rich, dark earth drinks in more
and more of the crystal drops,
becoming saturated and soggy.*

I feel soggy too. I've been drinking God's living water for such a long time now. But I know how fast it evaporates when the sun shines—when there are needs in others, when I give of that precious living water that is stored up in my soul. Sometimes just a look can drain me, or a prayer for a thirsty soul. So be prepared, my heart tells me—in and out of the rainy season.

Through the years I have learned to drink in—even when there is no apparent thirst, even though

I seem to be sated. Then the reservoir of life within me will always be adequate to supply my needs and the needs of others.

So I read the Word, and I sing to the Lord. I worship the King and praise the name of Jesus. By doing so, I keep my reservoir brimming over. And I expectantly look for opportunities to release some of the Lord's supply for someone else's need.

We are told to drink beyond our natural thirst—eight glasses of water a day—for our health. So it is with our spirit. We must drink in until we, like rain-soaked ground, are saturated to overflowing.

Jesus, you said, "Everyone who drinks this water will be thirsty again, but whoever drinks the water I give him will never thirst. Indeed, the water I give him will become in him a spring of water welling up to eternal life" (John 4:13–14). Saturate my spirit today so I will be ready to pour out your love to others. Amen.

My personal reflections

_____

_____

_____

_____

_____

_____

_____

_____

_____

_____

_____

_____

_____

_____

_____

_____

_____

_____

_____

_____

_____

7
Logs and Specks

> *You hypocrite, first take the log out of your own eye; and then you will see clearly enough to take the speck out of your brother's eye.*
>
> MATTHEW 7:5 *(NASB)*

Taking the "speck" out of our brother's eye is possible only after our "log" has first been removed. For example, eliminating the "log" of wrongly judging others allows us to overlook their flaws and see the true person. We fill them with hope and trust, and their own speck dissolves. For love judges purely, not critically. A good judge overcomes evil with righteousness, and uproots and supplants with love.

My dear friend songwriter and teacher Jimmy Owens once uprooted my fears with love. I had just received from the Lord "Easter Song." At the time I couldn't play the piano very well, but I wanted to play this song for Jimmy. It didn't seem right for

2nd Chapter of Acts and I thought he might use it on one of his records.

So I rose above my fears and played it, mistakes and all. Jimmy never mentioned the wrong notes. Instead, he said, "That is a great song! That's a 2nd Chapter of Acts song. You must keep it and record it." So we did. And it became one of our theme songs!

Now each time I sing "Easter Song" I am reminded that my brother didn't judge my lack of keyboard skills. Instead, he heard the song the way the Spirit gave it to me. The critical speck in my eye dissolved because there was none in his.

Father, forgive me for wrongly judging people. Help me to overlook the wrong notes they may play and instead listen to the music of their spirits—so they can be filled with hope. Amen.

My personal reflections

_____

_____

_____

_____

_____

_____

_____

_____

_____

_____

_____

_____

_____

_____

_____

_____

_____

_____

_____

_____

_____

_____

8
Little Bird

Shout for joy to the Lord, all the earth.
Worship the Lord with gladness; come
before him with joyful songs.

PSALM 100:1-2

It was a smoggy day typical of southern California. We were living in Wilmington where it always smells and every other back yard has an oil pump grinding away.

Our corner lot was a busy one, even though it was a residential area. On my walk that day, my attitude mirrored my surroundings. I was upset with the cars whizzing by and disgusted by the polluted air I had to breathe.

But then I heard a bird singing at the top of its lungs, just pouring out its heart. And the Spirit said to me,

> *That's how I want you to be, whatever the circumstance. Sing your heart out— it doesn't matter how you feel. And I*

*will use you like I am using that bird.
For the bird has drawn your attention
to me. And right now you are not
smelling the smog, or hearing the cars,
but your head has been lifted up by a
song. So you, too, will sing and lift up
the broken, give rest to the weary, and
draw people unto me. So, sing my little
bird! Sing, sing, sing!*

Lord, help me sing to you today—no matter what my
circumstance. May my song draw others' attention to
you, so that you can lift them up. Amen.

My personal reflections

_____

_____

_____

_____

_____

_____

_____

_____

_____

_____

_____

9
Changing Roles

Just as you received Christ Jesus as Lord, continue to live in him, rooted and built up in him, strengthened in the faith as you were taught, and overflowing with thankfulness.

COLOSSIANS 2:6–7

Why do I write? Because there's an empty page. We never had much to write on when I was little—paper was precious. I can still hear my mother saying, "Don't waste the paper," and she was right! We had very little of anything.

It's funny how as I've grown older I've started to see things more through my mother's eyes. I used to think, *Oh, if only Mother could see this*, or *If only Mother were alive, I could buy her that new dress . . . I could take care of her . . . she would be so proud of me.*

But now, rather than thinking of what I would like to have done for her, I feel more of what she must have felt. I wonder how many times her heart broke looking at us skinny kids, not knowing how

to show us a way out of poverty. Each set of eyes looking up at her cried deep down inside, *Help me become who I am to be.* And in every one of us, she saw a part of herself that might never be fulfilled. Because we lacked the financial opportunities to nurture our gifts, she knew she would never see them blossom and mature.

I look in the eyes of my brothers and sisters now, and I see their sorrows and their joys. Most of them have made it through to the other side, carrying their scars but never losing the joy of our mother. I see her in each one, and our desire to please her has not faded through time.

I see Mother in the grandchildren that she has never seen. In the way they raise their eyebrows and make funny faces . . .

The way they look you straightfaced in the eye and smile for no apparent reason . . .

The way they stop and look at nature as if it were just created . . .

Some of them hear the stars sing, some hear the trees grow. But all of them have been touched by her.

We were blessed to have such a loving mother, and I love seeing her life displayed through the grandchildren who never knew her.

And I wonder: Is Christ's nature evident in my character? Can my brothers and sisters in Christ see God's Spirit in me? Can the world see the eyes of Jesus in me as clearly as I can see my mother's face looking back at me in the mirror through my own eyes?

Jesus, be in my mirror. Live through me. For I long to look like you, be like you, live like you, love like you, and please you with all that I do. Amen.

My personal reflections

_____

_____

_____

_____

_____

_____

_____

_____

_____

_____

_____

_____

_____

_____

_____

10
Junk Mail

Give your servant a discerning heart…
to distinguish between right
and wrong.

1 Kings 3:9

When I was young, I would eagerly wait for the mailman to come down our road. I knew, of course, there wouldn't be anything for me. But every once in awhile Mother let me open some insignificant piece of mail, and that was a thrill for me.

I'm still the same. I love to go to the mailbox to see who wrote me. The junk mail I often find there—the meaningless assortment of stuffed envelopes—is not opened anymore. I have had enough of sweepstakes and messages like "You have won a car … $2,000 … a camera!" There's always a catch: to claim your prize you must drive 150 miles to look at property they want to sell you. And add to that all the other junk mail that tries to sell you stuff you don't need!

Even so, I still like to get the mail. Because I hope that by sifting through it, I will find a meaningful letter or even a parcel. We all like to receive gifts, especially the unexpected ones.

Sometimes our Sunday morning assemblies can include a little "junk mail" too. We must sift through it all and find the meaningful. For there are some beautifully wrapped boxes, disguised as Christ's gifts, that in reality are empty. We have all opened some of those boxes, because we are all curious and hungry for the truth. But it is important to discern which comes from Christ in us and learn to judge properly, not opening meaningless teachings or dogmatic doctrines.

We need to be able to hear His voice above all others. And if we listen carefully, this is what we hear Him say: "This is the way; walk in it" (Isaiah 30:21).

Today, Lord, I eagerly listen for your voice. I know that when I do stop long enough to listen to you, I always hear love, redemption, hope, wisdom, correction with purpose and comfort. I praise you for that. Amen.

My personal reflections

_____

_____

_____

_____

_____

_____

_____

_____

_____

_____

_____

_____

_____

_____

_____

_____

_____

_____

_____

_____

_____

_____

_____

_____

11
Stop and Let Go

If you obey my commands, you will remain in my love . . . I have told you this so that my joy may be in you and that your joy may be complete. My command is this: Love each other as I have loved you.

JOHN 15:10–12

As I look out on an audience I often see the weight on people's shoulders and the weariness in their eyes. Occasionally a feeling rises up inside me and I want to call out to them: "Look at Jesus! He is the only one who has taken all the cares of the world. Just give them to Him!"

Yet, I know frustration causes those thoughts and feelings, not peace or love, so I just stop . . . let go . . . and sing. And I watch the Holy Spirit do what He alone can do. He takes the song and uproots the foundation of fear in people's hearts. He sings joy into their weary faces and breaks the chains that have weighed down the saints.

And I didn't have to say a word! I obeyed Him and His command to "love one another . . . so your joy may be full."

Letting go, I leave every concert with *joy*! What a wonderful concept!

God, enable us to be obedient to you by quieting our frustrations and truly loving one another. Please let our gifts be used by your Spirit to bless, encourage and strengthen others. Amen.

My personal reflections

_____

_____

_____

_____

_____

_____

_____

_____

_____

_____

_____

_____

12
Come Away, My Beloved

He has taken me to the banquet hall,
and his banner over me is love.

SONG OF SONGS 2:4

I want to sit at your banqueting table, Lord, to taste of your goodness. But am I savoring all of your richness, or am I only having hors d'oeuvres instead of the feast?

Your invitation to the feast has been written in blood. It's easy to forget how much it cost you to send out invitations to all humanity, to each individual.

So I pray today that I will respond to your invitation to come and dine, to drink in your goodness, to behold your loveliness. I want to be empty of self as I pour out my gratitude for all you have done for me—for hearing my cry when loneliness was tearing me apart and sin was eating away at what was left of my eroded foundation.

How can I thank you enough for sending me that invitation and allowing my ears to hear you speak, "Come away, my beloved."

When I heard you say that, I knew for the first time what the word *precious* meant. For I became that precious gem that cost you so dearly. And in turn I could lay down my life so that you could become my precious Rock, my foundation of all hope—the Resurrection, the Living God, living your life in me!

Father, I want to feast on your goodness. Thank you for inviting me to the banquet. Let me hear again through these ears that may have become dull through time, "Come away, my beloved." Amen.

My personal reflections

_____

_____

_____

_____

_____

_____

_____

_____

_____

13
His Words

*Seek the Lord while he may be found;
call on him while he is near.*

ISAIAH 55:6

I don't think we ever are ready for the "big" events of life—like getting married or having children. I've often heard couples say before they decide to start a family, "We are just not ready for children yet." But often when a baby arrives they can't imagine life without him or her. The child opens new avenues of love in their hearts that they didn't know existed.

That is the way it is with God, too ... we are not ready for Him. We think if things get really bad, then we will turn to Him. Or maybe we will search for Him when we get older, or when we change—because we think we have to change ourselves before God will hear us.

It is only after we have gone through years of trying that we realize there is no way out and that we live in a hopeless situation. Only then do we

dare to call out to God for help. And what a giant surprise—He is there! He is there . . .

> *Like a shot in the dark,*
> *His words came flying,*
> *Straight to my heart,*
> *And stopped me crying.*
>
> *And speechless I stood,*
> *For words never could*
> *Explain what happened to me.*
>
> *Out of the night,*
> *Into the light,*
> *Where there is no shadow of turning.*
>
> *Where I was torn,*
> *Now I'm reborn.*

Lord, you said that I will find you when I seek you with all my heart (Jeremiah 29:13). Don't let me waste another day waiting for circumstances to be right. With all my heart, I want to know you. Amen.

My personal reflections

_____

_____

_____

_____

_____

_____

_____

_____

_____

_____

_____

_____

_____

_____

_____

_____

_____

_____

_____

14
Past Tense

My Grace is sufficient for you, for my power is made perfect in weakness.

II CORINTHIANS 12:9

Living God, Consuming Fire, burn the sin from my life,
Make your will my desire, take my life in your hands;
Purify me with your blood,
'Til I shine far brighter than purest gold in your eyes, Living God.

There are times when things I have done in the past come up and slap me in the face, stinging me with foolishness, taunting me that I should have known better. And a feeling of condemnation starts creeping all over me.

Then I stop and whisper: "O God, forgive me and take away this guilt. But if I must remember these things, please use them for your purposes."

Then God reminds me: He was there all the time, through it all, and there is no reason to hide anything from Him. After all, He knows what sin is—it killed Him. Christ knows rejection—His own Father abandoned Him for a time. Since God made us, He understands our pain, sorrow and grief. And He understands that the memory of small intimate sins can cripple us with guilt.

Love was the only thing that held Christ to the cross; the nails had no power over Him. But He allowed sin to kill Him. In doing so, He broke the gates of hell with His powerful love and glorious resurrection—and freed us from all of our sins. Now with the key of that love, we can unlock the sins of our past and bring them into His glorious light. There His holy, consuming fire can burn up the guilt brought on by their memory.

Lord, I need to trust you with my past, so I can trust you with my future. Help me today to surrender my past to you, so I'll never have to be afraid of it again. Amen.

My personal reflections

_____

_____

_____

_____

_____

_____

_____

_____

_____

_____

_____

_____

_____

_____

_____

_____

_____

_____

_____

_____

15
Clay Pots

O Lord, we are the clay, you are the potter; we are all the work of your hand.

ISAIAH 64:8

Scripture tells the story of how God sent the prophet Jeremiah to a potter's house. There he was to receive a message for the people of Israel, who had grown stubbornly idolatrous. As the potter worked with the clay at his wheel, the pot became marred in his hands. Consequently, he formed it into another pot, "shaping it as seemed best to him" (Jer. 18:4). This was the word of the Lord for his people: "O house of Israel, can I not do with you as this potter does?" (Jer. 18:6).

That is exactly what God has done with me. I was spoiled, touched by uncleanness in body and mind, only worth throwing away. But He loved me so much he took my sin-tainted flesh in His pure hands and remolded me, into a new vessel—clean, redeemed and set aside for His purposes.

Whatever God's purposes for me, no matter how grand or small, I realize I am not my own. I trust the Potter to do with me as it seems best to Him.

Lord, I may be an ordinary clay pot. But I was made for a place of significance in my world by you, the Master Potter. Help me accomplish whatever you want me to be and do today. Amen.

My personal reflections

_____

_____

_____

_____

_____

_____

_____

_____

_____

_____

_____

_____

16
Invisible Something

Whoever finds his life will lose it, and whoever loses his life for my sake will find it.

MATTHEW 10:39

It's all right to cry. To cry for others. To cry when we make a mistake. Crying stirs up our insides so we can get everything out and take a long look at ourselves—even if we don't like what we see.

Sometimes I cry while listening to music. It's not that I'm all that emotional; I just ache when I hear beauty, and it comes out my eyes. I've always been that way. I'm sure I was born with an ache in my heart.

My mother played the piano, and every once in awhile she would play a tune that would make me stop and listen—as if captured by an Invisible Something.

All through my life that Invisible Something wooed me, called me, helped me fly over storms in my life even when I didn't know I was flying. Then, all of a sudden, the presence seemed to leave me,

and that broke my heart. I began to cry and cry, for
I could see myself, and there was no beauty left in
me. I was in darkness, broken in every area, helpless
and weak. Every dream was hopeless, every
accomplishment dust. I was dying.

And then I heard that Invisible Something ring
out in me:

> *You must die to yourself and let me live
> through you, for I am your life. I am
> beauty. I am Jesus. And I will raise you
> from the dead. So don't be afraid to
> lose your life, for you will gain mine.*

I still need to die to certain things in my life. But
the new birth, the new beginning, happened when
I gave my life to Jesus. He continues to breathe His
newness into uncharted areas of my life. And I
stand in wonder as an invisible God becomes
visible through me—as I reach out, becoming
His hands and touching the needs in other
people's lives.

For that Invisible Something became flesh
when Jesus was born. And that same invisible
power that raised Jesus from the dead captures our
hearts and courses through us as we perform His
will on earth.

Almighty God, help me loosen my white-knuckled grip on my life. For in letting go of what I fear losing, I will find something exceedingly better—your life in me. Amen.

My personal reflections

_____

_____

_____

_____

_____

_____

_____

_____

_____

_____

_____

_____

_____

_____

_____

_____

17
Refuge From Fear

God hath not given us the spirit of fear; but of power, and of love, and of a sound mind.

2 TIMOTHY 1:7 (KJV)

Most of my life I have lived in fear—fear of others, even fear of myself. It has taken me forever to look into my heart and see that only love could break that fear.

And it took the gentle words of Jesus to let me know I could die to myself. He didn't say it wouldn't hurt, but He did say He would heal me. I was afraid to expose my darkest fears, but He said His light was alive and would dispel my fears and surround me with hope.

Fear is always harsh—so we must never be ruled by fear but by a sound mind and good judgment. We all must seek refuge from fear within God, so the harshness of this world does not take over our expression of love towards others. We all must rest in that gentle place before Him, learning to share what a hurting world will welcome without fear.

A thirsty land is afraid of storms,
But welcomes a gentle shower;
Sensitive eyes are afraid of bright
glaring light,
But welcome a gentle glow;
A hurting heart is afraid of harsh
accusations,
But welcomes a gentle word;
A broken body is afraid of all pain,
But welcomes a gentle hand;
A frozen forest is still afraid of fire,
But welcomes a gentle thaw.

God, you said that perfect love drives out fear. Help me
rest today in your perfect love, so that fear will have no
home in my heart. Amen.

My personal reflections

_____

_____

_____

_____

_____

_____

_____

_____

_____

18
Gratitude

Shout for joy to the Lord, all the earth. Worship the Lord with gladness; come before him with joyful songs. Know that the Lord is God. It is he who made us, and we are his; we are his people, the sheep of his pasture. Enter his gates with thanksgiving and his courts with praise; give thanks to him and praise his name. For the Lord is good and his love endures forever; his faithfulness continues through all generations.

PSALM 100

How many times have you looked out a window and seen the same trees, the same landscape . . . and yet been overwhelmed by the beauty? It is the same view, but continually your eyes catch a glimpse of something you've never seen before. And that beauty evokes gratitude from your heart.

Think of all the people who feel this joy and yet don't know whom is due their gratitude. I am grateful that I know the Creator. And I find myself thanking Him not only on my behalf, but on behalf of all those who don't know Him.

How kind our God is! What blessings He bestows on all of us. Our living, breathing planet is so beautiful, such a work of living art. My heart is also His handiwork. I pray that when God looks into my heart, He will see the changes that He has begotten, and it will bring Him joy.

But sometimes I am shortsighted. I see in me the same things as yesterday, the same landscape, without apparent change. And then I know it is time to turn my eyes to Jesus. Because when I do, I am filled with gratitude. I am overwhelmed by His love for me and His desire to make me whole by transforming me day to day, from glory to glory, for His glory.

Lord, thank you, thank you, thank you, for creating me and transforming me day to day to be more like you. Amen.

My personal reflections

_____
_____
_____
_____
_____
_____
_____
_____
_____
_____
_____
_____
_____
_____
_____
_____
_____
_____
_____
_____
_____
_____

19
Dreams

Now to him who is able to do immeasurably more than all we ask or imagine, according to his power that is at work within us, to him be glory in the church and in Christ Jesus throughout all generations, for ever and ever!

EPHESIANS 3:20–21

As a young girl, I dreamed my prince would one day come for me. It was a longing that never left my heart.

Back then, I didn't yet know that Jesus would return and take His bride to live with Him in heaven. I didn't know that Christ would become the reality of my life.

What a joy, what a surprise, when I came to know the Prince of Peace. That little girl's longing took flight in reality when I gave my life to Jesus at age twenty-three. My Prince arrived! And through my redemption, I came to see that besides being my Prince, He also is the Redeemer of Dreams.

Dancing shadows from the fire light
Call up past dreams still
seeking flight;
Those treasures dropped in our hearts
while young,
Have their own melody even
though unsung;
And from time to time we hear a
faint tune,
The longing to dance with the man in
the moon;
To rise up with wings and fly in
the sky,
These are the feelings that never should
die;
The past and the future have locked us
in place,
But each dream will take flight at the
end of the race.

Redeemer of Dreams, nurture in me your dreams for
my life. And give me faith to know that those dreams
really will take flight—in your timing. Amen.

My personal reflections

_____

_____

_____

_____

_____

_____

_____

_____

_____

_____

_____

_____

_____

_____

_____

_____

_____

_____

_____

_____

20
Look At Me

Look to the Lord and his strength; seek his face always.

PSALM 105:4

There is a constant in God's desire for us. No matter the circumstance . . . whether we are in a desert place filled with loneliness and despair, or in a place where His light has filtered through our understanding bringing peace, joy and rest. No matter what, that constant is: He always wants us to look at Him.

I remember teaching my young nephew to play racquetball. The first thing I told him was to keep his eye on the ball. I repeated over and over again, "Look at the ball. You must look at the ball so you can hit it!"

Later that day, my words still rang in my ears. And I thought, All my life the Lord has said to me, "Look at Me. You must look at Me so you can hit the mark, so you can be conformed into My image."

How many times do we consider our circumstances and then look to ourselves for

answers? After all, we've been taught all of our lives to think, I can do it! And so our focus is off, and we lose correct vision, for we are not looking at Him.

But this has been His cry to the human race from the beginning of time: "Look at Me. Look at Me, so you can live your life as I intended."

In my heart, Lord, I long to look at you. For I can't remember a time when you weren't there looking at me, watching over me, even when I didn't know you. Lord, may my eyes look to you first, so I will always be filled with peace no matter which way the wind blows. Amen.

My personal reflections

_____

_____

_____

_____

_____

_____

_____

_____

_____

_____

21
Shadows

*If I say, "Surely the darkness will hide
me and the light become night around
me," even the darkness will not be dark
to you; the night will shine like the day,
for darkness is as light to you.*

Psalm 139:11–12

O God, you are so much greater than the
feelings of inadequacy that I have running through
my body and mind today.

I see the beauty of the sun-drenched meadows,
and the shadows cast in among the trees. The
shadows are eerie, yet the beauty of the shade is
compelling to me.

Somehow that symbolizes how I feel about
myself today. A little afraid to have you see my
shadows. But nothing is truly hidden from you.
And yet, at times, I hide the way I really feel and
think, as though if you knew you would be aghast.

So in faith I give my shadows of doubt to you.
And I pray that they will become instead shades of

beauty and shelter for those uncomfortable feelings in me that need to find rest. Because there is no shadow of turning with you, I know I can lean on you to supply the peace that casts out fear.

Almighty God, you created the earth to constantly move, reaching out to the sun, submitting to its full rays for a time, and letting the shadows change as they may. May I be as willing to let your light play upon my soul. Amen.

My personal reflections

_____

_____

_____

_____

_____

_____

_____

_____

_____

_____

_____

_____

22
Fallible Fruit

I am the vine; you are the branches. If a man remains in me and I in him, he will bear much fruit; apart from me you can do nothing.

JOHN 15:5

How do I give my life away? Not by merely draining out my tangible resources; that would be too easy. Done once, and then it's all over. No, my life is in Christ, and He is my Source. I must bring myself to Him, for He alone can bless and break my life to feed the hungry in the isolated places.

But I don't like those isolated places. I'd much rather be in the marketplace, getting what I want to eat when I want it and then giving to the hungry out of my wealth. Somehow I don't see any dying to self in that way, though. Or even any need to cast my care on Him. So, that must not be true life.

Being my own person, even giving my own things away, is not life. He is the vine, we are the branches. Fruit grows on the branches to be harvested and eaten. But oh, how we worry if no one comes to harvest or to feed.

We seem to have a knack for force-feeding our fruit to others so it won't go to waste! But have we ever thought that maybe the fruit isn't good enough yet for consumption? Perhaps it needs another "go around" to become sweet? We forget that God in His wisdom knows the condition of our soil and sometimes wants us to let our fruit drop to nourish the ground and to strengthen the yield for the next season.

He is after all Lord of the soil too. And most of us have depleted, undernourished soil, because we give and do for God instead of His giving and doing through us.

"What have I done for God?" No, no, no.

"What has God done through me?" That is the question we must ask. For every time He flows through us, we become less, and He becomes greater.

Lord of the Harvest, you are the vine that nourishes the fruit my branches will bear. Grant me deeply-rooted faith in your process, your timing, and your purposes. Amen.

My personal reflections

_____

_____

_____

_____

_____

_____

_____

_____

_____

_____

_____

_____

_____

_____

_____

_____

_____

_____

_____

_____

23
Riding The Wind

It's rainy today. Lovely, gray with bursting colors. It's the last hurrah of green before the fall colors take hold. I love the calm after a heavy rain. It stirs something in me—a longing, a dying, a rebirth, a complex matrix.

My room is exactly the same as it was yesterday, but the shadowing is all different. And how easily my attitude is changed by the amount of light that floods into my room. I enjoy every shade, every sunbeam, every cast and hue. A part of me wants to run up and flatly touch each dimension. The shadows and light become more concrete than the walls or furniture. Sometimes it feels as though my room has become a clear ice cube where everything is frozen in its place by light. And somehow I can

look into it and see myself—a person, female, child, woman; timeless, endless and yet so frail.

I stop and wonder, what are my needs anyway? What are my desires? I think "to be whole" would be my answer today. Whole in the complete sense. Where spirit is more "concrete" than flesh. Where thought is felt and not locked in the mind struggling to find a way to express itself.

There must be more to the wind than invisibleness. And yet the Word says that we can't grasp it—not with our hands anyway.

Yet, I have been caught up by the Spirit wind many times and have flown like a hawk through impossible passageways. I feel as though I have ridden the wind right through the walls of sorrow and grief where the brokenhearted are locked up.

Many times while I am singing, I feel I am part of the wind's invisibleness. From my singular perspective on stage I can see the words fall on people's hearts and watch their faces soften.

And yes, I want to bring those hurting people out, one by one, and watch them feel freedom as the wind of God's Spirit blows away their shackles of captivity.

Holy Spirit, renew me. Refresh me. This day, help me catch the wind of hope and learn to soar with newfound wings. Amen.

My personal reflections

_____

_____

_____

_____

_____

_____

_____

_____

_____

_____

_____

_____

_____

_____

_____

_____

_____

_____

_____

_____

_____

24
We Are What We Behold

Let us fix our eyes on Jesus, the author and perfecter of our faith.

HEBREWS 12:2

2nd Chapter of Acts, which consisted of my brother, Matthew, my sister, Nelly, and me, often toured with Barry McGuire. We learned a lot from Barry. Between songs he often talked to the audience about practical aspects of Christianity. For example, I remember him talking about friendship. He said,

> Have you ever noticed that when two girls become really close friends they start looking like each other? They wear the same color nail polish, have their hair cut the same, wear the same outfits, and even like the same boys? That applies to guys too. It's human nature to become like the people we hang out with, so pick your friends carefully. More importantly, hang out with Jesus and you will become like Him.

Here's the key principle I learned from Barry:
We are what we behold.

> *Behold the world—we become like the world.*
> *Behold others—we become like them.*
> *Behold ourselves—we become selfish.*
> *Behold Jesus—we become like Jesus.*

Dear brothers and sisters, let us keep our eyes on Jesus.

Lord, help me keep my gaze on you, and so become more like you today. Amen.

My personal reflections

_____

_____

_____

_____

_____

_____

_____

_____

_____

_____

25
Drinking & Splashing

Whoever believes in me, as the Scripture has said, streams of living water will flow from within him.

JOHN 7:38

A squirrel has discovered our birdbath.

It's been there filled with fresh water for about ten months. But the squirrel has finally figured out how to get up the pedestal and onto the bowl. He could smell that water for a long time. Then one day he got a good running start, jumped to the rim of the bowl, put his face in the water and drank to his heart's content.

I'm sure the squirrel knew all along that it was a birdbath . . . he had seen birds drinking and splashing and calling others to join in. But he was a squirrel after all . . . and have you ever heard of a squirrelbath?

So he would watch, not realizing that sometimes the birds were calling to him, for they sensed he must be thirsty, too.

Months passed, and the birds kept coming to drink at the birdbath. All the while, the squirrel searched for a meager supply of water here and there—in the leaves that held some raindrops or on the grass that had been freshly watered. But to sit and drink in all the water he wanted was only a dream.

Summer hit late but hot, and things began to dry up. So when all the hidden corners that held some drops of water for the squirrel came up empty, he became desperate, wandering around the pedestal until at last he found the courage and strength to make it to the top to taste the fresh water. Now he goes every day as though it were nothing—easy as pie.

Isn't that the way it is with the new things from God, the gifts He gives? When we finally come to our senses and find the courage to use them, they become a natural, normal way of living.

I can smell the fresh water the Lord has for me. I can almost feel the refreshing dampness around me. But sometimes like the squirrel I don't quite know how to plunge in.

That's when God shows me how to take another leap of faith. And before you know it I'm drinking and splashing again—exulting in the newness and refreshment I seek, the anointing of grace I need.

Lord, I want so much to taste your living water. Although I know it's abundantly there for me, sometimes I'm so afraid I instead scavenge about for meager drops here and there. Give me the courage to take a leap of faith and dive into the fullness of your grace. Amen.

My personal reflections

_____

_____

_____

_____

_____

_____

_____

_____

_____

_____

_____

_____

_____

_____

26
Woman At The Well

If the Son sets you free, you will be free indeed.

JOHN 8:36

Many Samaritans believed in Jesus because of the testimony of the woman He spoke with at the well. She said, "He told me everything I ever did," (John 4:39). Her words led them to Jesus.

After they spent time with Him they said to the woman, "We no longer believe just because of what you said; we have heard for ourselves, and we know that this man really is the Savior of the world," (John 4:42).

We must tell what Christ has done in our lives. We simply must say that Christ has changed us and, like the woman at the well, He has told us all we have done—our sins that have caused hurt, pain and guilt.

People may believe us and see that we are free. But that won't change them or set them free—we must lead them to Jesus, for . . .

> *He takes the weak ones,*
> *He takes the broken;*
> *He takes the simple*
> *To confound the wise.*
>
> *He takes the darkness,*
> *He takes the sorrow;*
> *He takes the confusion,*
> *And breaks the lies.*
>
> *No one else could ever do it,*
> *No one else as pure as He;*
> *No one else could ever do it,*
> *Cast our sins into the sea.*

Loving Father, forgive me for hoarding your great gift of salvation. Open my eyes to those in my world who are dying to be free of their sin. Help me say the words that will lead them to you. Amen.

My personal reflections

_____

_____

_____

_____

_____

_____

_____

_____

_____

_____

_____

_____

_____

_____

_____

_____

_____

_____

_____

_____

_____

27
His Light

Let your light shine before men, that they may see your good deeds and praise your Father in heaven.

MATTHEW 5:16

Have you ever noticed how dramatically and drastically colors change on a cloudy day when the sun finds a hole to shine through? Everything seems to come to life when the sun shines. Colors are more vivid, and all of nature seems much more approachable.

Our human nature is that way, too. When we are "cloudy" or blue, others are not apt to feel comfortable with us, so they move away. There seems to be a shield or a wall that keeps us from touching each other where there might be a need. Most of the time we are not even aware that we are shrouded in these cloudy extensions of ourselves. But by the end of the day we do feel unsettled deep inside.

Praise God that He can touch us where we feel, that He uses His peace as a barometer in our lives.

Then, if we are sensitive to our own hearts, we can hear Him say, "Come, bask in My light." As we do, He chases the clouds away.

That doesn't mean He chases the circumstances away. But He clears the air so we can see Him and are then able to face any problem, no matter how difficult, with faith that He will see us through. Then, we are more approachable, and His light shines through us giving others hope.

Remember, God's light never goes out; He is always shining. And the lying prince of darkness can never, ever, put Him out.

Committing ourselves to be in God's presence, we allow Him to prepare our hearts. Then He can shine through us to others and, in turn, enable us to recognize and receive His light from those around us.

Shine on, Lord. Shine through me today, for the sake of my sisters and brothers. Amen.

My personal reflections

_____

_____

_____

_____

_____

_____

_____

_____

_____

_____

_____

_____

_____

_____

_____

_____

_____

_____

_____

_____

_____

_____

28
Forgive

Then came Peter to him and said, Lord, how oft shall my brother sin against me, and I forgive him? Til seven times? Jesus saith unto him, I say not unto thee, until seven times: but until seventy times seven.

MATTHEW 18:21–22 (KJV)

I have no right not to forgive seventy times seven. That's a lot, but the Lord says I must forgive from my heart. That means no bitter, venomous or slanted words should come out towards anyone, or else forgiveness hasn't taken over all of my heart.

Countless times after I've forgiven someone, the bite of bitterness stings me at our next encounter, taking me by surprise. Then once again I bring it to the Lord, and He reminds me that forgiveness isn't a feeling—it is a choice. So I keep choosing to come to Him until my whole heart is free through the power of forgiveness. As my friend Stormie Omartian says, forgiveness doesn't make the other person right, it simply sets you free.

My Lord, as you forgive me, help me to forgive. I have no purity outside of you, no strength, no hope, or goals ... empty, selfish, lazy, pleasure-seeking. O Lord, I can't find an end to that list of self, but you nailed that list and my hopelessness to the cross ... thank you. Amen.

My personal reflections

_____

_____

_____

_____

_____

_____

_____

_____

_____

_____

_____

_____

_____

_____

29
Precious Encounter

The body is a unit, though it is made up of many parts; and though all its parts are many, they form one body. So it is with Christ.

1 CORINTHIANS 12:12

In a concert ministry where you constantly meet new people, it's easy to start lumping them into categories. But the Lord gave me a key years ago that has helped me keep my perspective. When I meet a believer, I realize I am meeting part of Christ I have never seen or known before. How precious that is!

You see, Jesus met countless people, too. He didn't have a dressing room to run to after He spoke, or a curtain to put an end to the evening. Afterwards, I'm sure He was asked many questions. Some intimate and personal—from those who dared to seek help. Others general—to clarify a point their group was debating. Of course, He got worn and weary and pulled Himself away from the crowds from time to time.

But what an example of love and patience Jesus is to me. He has helped me go out in a crowd after a concert without fear of what people may ask or say. Instead, I go with joy, knowing I am going to see a part of Christ I have never known before and hoping I will impart the comfort of Christ to others.

Lord, help me see you in each person I meet today. Amen.

My personal reflections

_____

_____

_____

_____

_____

_____

_____

_____

_____

_____

_____

_____

30
After Christmas

*My eyes have seen your salvation,
which you have prepared in the sight
of all people, a light for revelation to
the Gentiles and for glory to your
people Israel.*

LUKE 2:30–31

I didn't look forward to Christmas last year.
Even when it came my heart wasn't in it. Probably
because I had worked hard and was done before
the year was. November required of me the total
discipline of rising from depleted desires, but I
knew commitment at that level was what my
atrophied thinking process needed.

Despite my lethargy, spiritual realities didn't
change—holiness was still holiness . . . beauty, peace
and joy were still beauty, peace and joy. But I felt
the inner boundary, the line that separates me from
this world and the next, being tested and played
upon by the Great Musician to see if I were in tune.

So I learned to look beyond and through heat waves that cause optic distortion by keeping my eyes closer to the ground in front of my toes. Each small step was then visible to me and kept me true to my commitments. I'm not talking about duty or religious calisthenics, guilt or false pressure. Rather, I'm speaking of narrowing and honing down the nebulous future into the essence of each moment. Discovering the second that wasn't there a second ago, without letting dreams, hopes, peace, love or joy die.

And so, I found myself in the new year, wondering how I would feel about Christmas this year. Yet something told me that Christmas would never come until that inner boundary, or fine string, that separates me from this world and the next was played upon and played upon, until I rang out the melodious words of God's heart.

That's all God's ever wanted me to do from the first time I laid my bewildered eyes upon Him. Without my knowing the full meaning of our encounter, these unspoken words were translated through His eyes: *Let me live through you*. It rang true in my heart, and I knew my search was over. Yet I didn't know how to do what God asked until I was told I must die to myself and then be born again.

Lord, I can't thank you enough, for there is no equation, no language, no formula that can explain the joy of being born again. Master Musician, keep singing your life-song into my being, setting my life apart for your purposes in this world and for your glory in the next. Amen.

My personal reflections

_____

_____

_____

_____

_____

_____

_____

_____

_____

_____

_____

_____

_____

_____

_____

Music by Annie Herring

Flying Lessons

Waiting for My Ride to Come

There's a Stirring

All That I Am

Glimpses

Music by 2nd Chapter of Acts

Mansion Builder

Rejoice

How the West Was One, Vol. I and II

Roar of Love

Singer Sower

Night Light

Far Away Places

Hymns I

Hymns II

Hymns Instrumental

20: 1972–1992 Box Set

Hymns Collection Box Set

New from Annie Herring!

Glimpses

Share Annie Herring's special insights into our comforting God through the songs of her newest recording. *Glimpses* resounds with the truth that God is always with us, invisible yet ever-present.

Glimpses—Coming to your local Christian bookstore October '96.